HEARING-EAR DOGS

BY PHYLLIS RAYBIN EMERT

EDITED BY DR. HOWARD SCHROEDER
Professor in Reading and Language Arts
Dept. of Elementary Education
Mankato State University

**PRODUCED & DESIGNED BY
BAKER STREET PRODUCTIONS**

CRESTWOOD HOUSE

LIBRARY OF CONGRESS CATALOGING IN PUBLICATION DATA

Emert, Phyllis Raybin.
  Hearing ear dogs.

  (Working dogs)
  SUMMARY: Discusses the history, training, uses, and breeds of dogs
who work with the deaf, and lists hearing ear dog programs in the United
States.
  1. Hearing ear dogs--Juvenile literature. (1. Hearing ear dogs.) I.
Schroeder, Howard. II. Baker Street Productions. III. Title. IV. Series.
HV2509.E48   1985   636.7'088   85-12841
ISBN 0-89686-283-6 (lib. bdg.)

International Standard	**Library of Congress**
Book Number:	**Catalog Card Number:**
Library Binding 0-89686-283-6	85-12841

ILLUSTRATION CREDITS

Peter Hornby: Cover, 4, 7, 8, 11, 13, 17, 19, 27
Canine Companions for Independence: 14, 20, 41
Ron Dickey: 18
Judy Savage: 23, 24, 29, 30, 33, 36, 38-39, 46
San Francisco SPCA Hearing-Dog Program: 34, 42-43

CRESTWOOD HOUSE
Hwy. 66 South, Box 3427
Mankato, MN 56002-3427

Table of contents

The author would like to thank the following people and organizations for their help and cooperation:
Gay Currier of Canine Companions for Independence in Santa Rosa, California;
Deanna Carter of the West Boylston, Massachusetts Hearing-Ear Dog Program;
Ralph Dennard of the San Francisco SPCA Hearing Dog Program.
Additional thanks go to Dogs for the Deaf in Jacksonville, Oregon, and American Humane in Denver, Colorado.
A very special thank you to Larry Emert.

1.

Dan and Mollie

Dan and his wife, Jean, were a happy couple. Dan had worked for twenty-five years as a bus driver. Jean was a clerk in an office. They lived alone in a small house.

Jean was worried about her husband. Lately, Dan had been acting strange. He barely spoke to her. Just the other day, Jean asked him to answer the door when she was washing her hair. He kept working on his model ship and ignored her.

Jean felt there might be something wrong with Dan.

Jean wasn't the only one who felt something was wrong. Joe, their neighbor, often yelled at Dan from his backyard to come over and watch the baseball game. But Dan kept right on working in the garden, never saying a word.

"What's wrong with him?" Joe thought angrily. "If he won't speak to me, I won't bother with him either."

Dan was even having trouble at work. Some of the riders on his bus had complained. "I asked him to stop the bus and let me off at Oak Street," one woman said. "He just kept on going."

"I pulled the buzzer so he'd let me off at First Street," a man said. "He didn't stop. I had to walk four blocks out of my way and I was late for work."

Dan's boss was worried, too. Dan had always been one of his best men. The boss told him to go see a doctor.

Dan went home early that day. He was watching television when Jean walked in. The TV was so loud that Jean had heard it down the block. She went to the set and turned it down. "It's too loud, Dan," said Jean. "Are you deaf or something?"

All of a sudden, the pieces fit together in Jean's mind. He wasn't ignoring her, or Joe, or his customers. He just couldn't hear them!

Jean and Dan had a long talk about his problem. Dan said he knew he was losing his hearing, and it scared him. He had kept thinking that it might get better, but it hadn't.

Together Dan and Jean went to an ear doctor. While Dan was being tested, Jean sat in the waiting room. A young woman walked in with a little girl about two-years-old. The woman had a small dog on a leash. Jean saw that the dog had a bright orange collar.

"Why couldn't she leave that dog in the car?" thought Jean. The dog sat quietly next to the woman who began reading a book. The little girl played near-by. "At least, the dog is well-behaved," Jean said to herself.

All of a sudden, a loud scream pierced the air. The little girl had tripped and hurt herself on the edge of the table. She began to cry. But her mother kept reading her book.

As Jean watched, the little dog ran to the child. Then it raced back to the woman, jumping up on her legs. As the woman looked up, the dog ran back to the girl. When the woman saw her daughter sobbing, she hurried to comfort her. Then she praised and hugged the dog.

"Amazing," thought Jean. "I should have known. The woman is deaf, and the dog let her know the child was crying."

After awhile, the doctor called Jean and Dan into his office together. "I'm sorry to say that Dan is losing his hearing," he said. "We don't know why, but soon he will be completely deaf. There's nothing we can do."

As his hearing got worse, Dan's life changed. He had to give up his job as a bus driver. He stayed home all day while Jean was at work. He felt lonely and helpless. "You don't know what it's like, Jean," he said. "Plug up your ears with cotton for a few hours. See how it is living in total silence."

Jean walked outside. "How can I help him?" she thought, as she watched the kids across the street with their dog. The children threw a stick and the dog raced to grab it. "Cute dog," Jean thought as she turned to go in. "Wait a minute," she said out loud. "The dog. Yes, of course, the dog who helped the deaf woman!" Jean raced inside to tell Dan all about the dog she had seen in the doctor's office.

The dog across the street reminded Jean of the deaf woman in the doctor's office.

The next day, Jean got the phone number of a nearby hearing-dog program. She called and they mailed Dan an application.

"What's nice about this program is that you'll be getting a stray dog from the pound," Jean said slowly, as Dan tried to read her lips. "You'll be giving the dog a new life."

Dan filled out the forms. He hoped that the dog could be trained to alert him to the sounds of the alarm clock, the doorbell, the smoke alarm, and the teakettle.

Dan's application was looked over by people who worked for the hearing-dog program. Then they talked to Dan in his home. Dan was asked many questions, especially about dogs. Finally, they checked to see if he had a fenced yard.

One day Jean came home from work to find Dan smiling. "The hearing-dog program accepted me," he said. "I'm on the waiting list for a dog."

Over the next few months, Dan passed the time reading books. He learned how to groom, exercise,

Dan read books on how to care for a dog.

feed, and care for a dog. Then a letter came in the mail telling him about his own hearing-ear dog. Her name was Mollie. She was a small, mixed-breed terrier. A picture of Mollie was enclosed. That night, Jean heard Dan whistling as he got ready for bed.

The big day finally arrived. The trainer was going to bring Mollie to the house. The day before, Dan had gone shopping with Jean. He picked out dog food, a dog dish, a dog bed, brushes, combs, and even a rawhide bone.

Dan met Mollie at the door. She ran up and licked Dan's face. Then Mollie went to explore the rest of the house. For Dan, it was love at first sight! During the next few days, the trainer taught Dan how to work with Mollie. Then he left them alone. After a few weeks of getting used to each other, they would become a team.

Mollie slept beside Dan's bed at night. In the morning, when the alarm clock went off, Mollie jumped up on the bed. She licked Dan's face until he woke up. "Okay, Mollie, I'm awake," he said.

Mollie sat quietly as Dan got out of bed. "Good dog, Mollie," he said as he patted her on the head. He always remembered to praise the dog. Sometimes he gave her a special food treat.

"I'll put on the water to make coffee," he said to Jean as she went to take a shower.

A few minutes later, while he was shaving, Mollie rushed into the bathroom. She jumped up on Dan, rushed out, and then ran back to Dan. He followed the dog into the kitchen and saw the steam coming from the teakettle. "Good girl, Mollie," he said as he gave her a treat. Dan smiled as he poured coffee for Jean and himself.

Before Mollie came, he would stand around waiting for the water to boil. One time, he walked out of the room and then forgot that the stove was on. A fire had almost started and the teakettle was ruined.

As Jean went to work, she kissed Dan goodbye. "Don't forget that the repairman is coming today to fix the TV," she said.

"No problem," Dan said.

He was hard at work on the sails of his model ship when the doorbell rang. In a flash, Mollie ran to the door, then to Dan. She jumped up, pushing him with her paws, and darted back to the door. "It must be the repairman, Mollie," he said. "Good girl." He patted her on the head.

Dan thought back in time. He had once waited all day long for the plumber to come fix the sink. He sat for hours looking out the front window so he wouldn't miss him. He left for a few minutes to make a sandwich in the kitchen. When he got back, he looked out to see the plumber's truck driving away. The plumber had left a note on his doorknob. "Sorry, you were out when I came." Dan had never felt so helpless.

Every day Dan took Mollie out for a walk or to play. She had her own collar, which said she was a hearing-ear dog. The kids in the neighborhood came over to play with Dan and Mollie. Mollie loved running after balls. Sometimes she caught them in her mouth while the ball was still in the air.

Jean came home from work one day while Dan was outside playing with the dog. "It's so good to see him laugh and smile again," she thought to herself. "He's not afraid anymore."

"Hi, Jean," Dan said. "Mollie and I are going over to Joe's to watch the ballgame. We'll be back for dinner."

That night Jean walked into the living room. Dan and Mollie were curled up together on the couch taking a nap. Mollie had her head on Dan's chest. "You're a good girl, Mollie," Jean said softly. The dog perked up her ears and opened her eyes. Looking at Jean, she thumped her tail in thanks a few times. Then Mollie yawned and went back to sleep.

Mollie changed Dan's life.

2.

Hearing-dogs in history

Dogs have been used by some deaf people for quite awhile. In San Francisco in the 1940's, John Collier trained Jokko to be a hearing-ear dog for two deaf ladies. One night, Jokko sensed something was wrong. He smelled leaking gas in their bedroom and woke up the women just in time. The dog saved their lives.

In Ohio in 1946, a dog was trained to let his deaf mistress know when the telephone was ringing. When the "party" phone rang two times, the dog knew the call was for his mistress. Then he raced to his owner and pawed at her dress. The dog ignored all the other telephone rings.

A real program to train dogs for the deaf didn't begin until many years later. In 1974, a deaf woman lost a dog she had trained to alert her to a doorbell or knock at the front door. She asked the Minnesota Society for the Prevention of Cruelty to Animals (SPCA) for help. The SPCA agreed to train a new dog.

Agnes McGrath, a dog trainer at the SPCA, started a hearing-dog project to replace the woman's dog. They soon trained and placed several more dogs with other deaf people. The program grew quickly to meet the needs of deaf people in the area.

Hearing-dog programs have given new freedom to deaf people all over the United States.

The SPCA turned the program over to the larger American Humane Association in 1976. Today, the Association no longer trains and places hearing-ear dogs. Instead, it provides people with information about the seventeen hearing-ear dog programs across the United States. (Over three million Americans are deaf. Another fourteen million have some hearing loss).

3.

Requirements

A hearing-ear dog should be alert, friendly, and full of energy. It should also be smart and have an even temperament. Hearing dogs can be either male or female. They start training when they are about six to

Hearing-dogs start training when they are young.

twenty-four months old. "We don't want them much younger, because it takes more time for them to become good companions," says Ralph Dennard, Director of the San Francisco SPCA Hearing-Dog Program. "An older dog may have bad habits that are hard to break."

Some programs let the deaf person ask for a special breed or size of dog. Most people want small to medium-sized dogs. They're easier to care for in an apartment or small home. The San Francisco program only picks dogs up to forty pounds. Most hearing-dog programs choose dogs from local animal shelters. All are homeless strays who would, otherwise, be "put to sleep."

Mixed-breed dogs

Mixed-breed terriers and poodles have often been used with success as hearing-ear dogs. The demonstration dog at the San Francisco program is a mixed terrier named Penny. The word, terrier, comes from the Latin word, terra, meaning earth. These dogs love to dig. They were first used to follow foxes and badgers into their underground homes.

Terriers come from the British Isles and date back to at least 55 B.C. There are twenty-two kinds of terriers. All have their own special look and color. Most are small to medium in size.

Mixed-breed poodles are very intelligent, gentle, and

loving. They learn things quickly and take directions well. Poodles never shed hair, so they make good indoor dogs. Mixed poodles are many different sizes, shapes, and colors. It depends on the breed with which they're matched.

Mixed-breed spaniels, dachshunds, and German shepherds have also been used as hearing-ear dogs.

Purebred dogs

Canine Companions for Independence in Santa Rosa, California uses only purebred Schipperkes, Corgis, and Border Collies as hearing-ear dogs. These dogs are hard workers, dependable, and small in size.

The Schipperke (pronounced skip'-er-key) comes from Belgium and is a small version of the black sheepdog. The name means "little captain" in Flemish. They were first used hundreds of years ago as watch-dogs and as guards for workmen.

Schipperkes are solid black with a short, thick body. They're very alert and gentle to children. The Schip's tail is cut to an inch or less in length. Its coat is thick and rough to the touch. They have long, thick hair around the neck, called a ruff. The Schip's are nine to twelve inches (22.86 - 30.48 cm) tall and weigh twelve to eighteen pounds (5.44 - 8.17 kg). Many Schipperkes live to an old age of sixteen years or more.

There are two kinds of Welsh Corgis, the Cardigan

and the Pembroke. They're named after counties in Wales where they were first bred. These dogs are sturdy little animals with short legs and long bodies. Their heads look like foxes. The Cardigans have a long, bushy tail. The Pembroke has a tiny tail or no tail at all.

The Corgis are very intelligent, alert, and friendly. They are easy to care for and make excellent house pets. Corgis are eager learners and willing to please. Their coats are thick and rough, and of medium length. Corgis are ten to twelve inches (25.40 - 30.48 cm) tall at the shoulder. They weigh from fifteen to thirty-five pounds

Welsh Corgis are excellent hearing-ear dogs.

(6.80 - 15.88 kg). They're between thirty-six and forty-four inches (91.44 - 111.76 cm) long from the nose to the tip of the tail.

Pembrokes are red, sable, fawn, black, or tan in color, with or without white markings. Cardigans are usually red and sable in color. They also come in blue merle (blue and grey mixed with black), tri-color (white, black, and tan), and red or black brindle (a mixture of dark and light hairs).

Corgis make good house pets.

Border Collies are very smart dogs.

Border Collies also come from the British Isles. They are best known for herding sheep, cattle, pigs, and poultry. The dogs are trained to work alone or with their masters. They are able to follow whistle, voice, and hand signals.

Border Collies are speedy, alert, and full of energy. They're very intelligent and follow directions well. Most are about eighteen inches (45.72 cm) high at the shoulder. They weigh from thirty to forty-five pounds (13.61 - 20.41 kg). The coat of the Border Collie is very thick and curly. They're mostly black, with a white band around the neck. They also have white markings on the chest, face, feet, and the tip of the tail.

4.

Training methods

There are seventeen hearing-dog programs in the United States today. Their goals are the same. They all train and place dogs with deaf people. However, each program may differ in the way the dogs are taught. What follows is a general description of training hearing-ear dogs. The programs mentioned by name are described in more detail.

Pictured above are deaf students with their hearing-ear dogs at Canine Companions for Independence.

Signal dogs

At Canine Companions for Independence, hearing-ear dogs are called Signal Dogs. This program breeds their own purebred puppies. Only Border Collies, Schipperkes, and Welsch Corgis are bred as Signal Dogs.

At seven to eight weeks of age, the pups are checked for temperament and how they respond to people and commands. Alert, smart, and friendly puppies go on to the next step in their training. The other pups are placed in good homes in the community.

Puppy raisers

The puppies are placed in foster homes until they are old enough to begin advanced training. The foster family gives them love, care, and attention. Canine Companions for Independence (CCI) calls it their Puppy Raising Program. Young boys and girls, as well as adult men and women, are puppy raisers. The pup sleeps in the puppy raisers' bedroom and they go places together.

CCI has puppy classes every two weeks for the raiser to attend. The classes teach basic puppy care. Special problems of deaf people are also discussed.

The puppy raiser is the dog's first trainer. The pup is taught as many as thirty-six house and street commands. They include obedience commands such as "sit," "down," "stand," and "come." Other commands are "say hello" (the pup rests its head on the trainer's lap) and "go in" (the pup goes under the table or out of the way). They're also taught "quiet" and "go to bed." At the command, "get dressed," the puppy slips into its collar and backpack while the trainer holds it up.

The puppy raiser takes the pup to many different places. This gets the puppy used to meeting new people. The raisers teach the pups how to have good manners at all times.

People who can't take a pup into their house, but still want to take part in the program, are called puppy socializers. These people come to CCI to play with young pups that are waiting to go to foster homes. Puppy socializers groom the dogs and take them on walks.

Dogs are usually returned to CCI when they reach twelve to fifteen months of age.

Animal shelters

Sometimes personal pets are trained to be hearing-ear dogs. But most hearing-dog programs choose their dogs from local animal shelters.

Dogs who would soon be put to sleep are "rescued" by hearing-dog trainers. Trainers look for dogs that are young, friendly, alert, and small to medium-size. Sometimes a veterinarian will go with the trainer to help pick out the dogs. The vet can usually tell at a glance whether the dog has any medical problems.

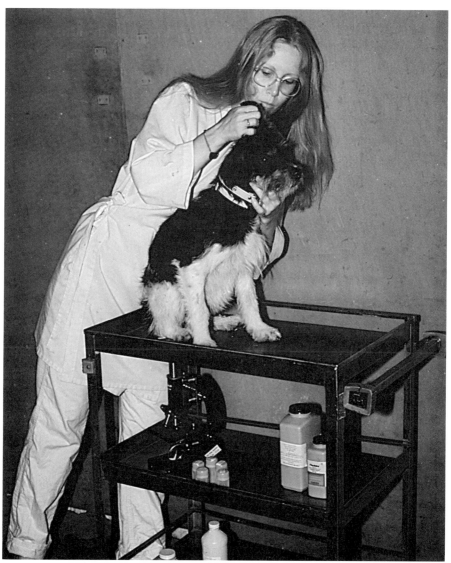

A veterinarian checks to see if a dog has any medical problems.

Qualifying tests

The dogs from the shelters are given a series of tests to see if they will qualify as hearing-ear dogs. The most important test is for awareness of sound. The trainer may play a tape of a baby crying, or of a buzzer on an alarm clock. The dog is watched to see if it tries to find out where the sound is coming from. A dog which ignores the sounds will not pass the test.

Another test deals with wanting to "work." At the San Francisco SPCA Hearing Dog Program, the trainer throws a ball and the dog is told to get it. "If it doesn't bring it back, the dog should, at least, go toward it,"

This puppy is being tested for sound awareness.

says Ralph Dennard, Director of the Program.

There are also tests for curiosity. At San Francisco, when the dog isn't looking, a windup toy which makes noise is started. The dog is expected to look over the toy. It shouldn't be afraid or walk away from it. In other programs, the dog is expected to look at itself in a mirror.

The dog must also be friendly with people and have an even temperament. Nervous, shy, or growling dogs don't pass this test. San Francisco also tests the dogs for their ability to accept pain. The trainer pinches the animal to see how it reacts. If the dog bites or snaps, it fails the test. The leash may be jerked hard to see if the dog gets upset. The dog should forgive the trainer and not get angry.

Finally, the dog is forced to lie down by someone it doesn't know. This shows if the dog will accept the trainer's commands. A dog who panics or gets upset is cut from the program.

Ralph Dennard states that only half of the dogs at the San Francisco program pass all of these tests. Those who pass go on to the veterinarian. This animal doctor gives each animal a complete checkup to make sure it is in good health.

Some programs keep the healthy dogs by themselves for up to ten days. This is to be sure no disease appears suddenly which might harm other dogs. During this time, the dogs are walked and played with by the trainers.

Obedience Training

Most programs take three to six months to train a hearing-ear dog. Obedience is an important part of that training. The dogs are first taught to heel on a leash. They learn to walk along with the trainer on the left side. Dogs are also taught to "sit," "lie down," "stay," and "come."

At CCI, the commands first taught by the puppy raisers are practiced again and again. More are added as training goes on. At the West Boylston, Massachusetts Hearing-Dog Program, dogs are taken into town to visit stores and businesses. They get used to being in public places. They see new people and are exposed to different situations. Other hearing-dog groups have similar programs.

Sign Language

Deaf people use their hands to talk to each other. This is called sign language. There is a special hand sign for each letter of the alphabet. Some hand signs actually look like the letter they're suppose to be. Some do not. To sign, the hand is closed into a loose fist. The first two fingers are straightened out to make a "V." That's the letter "V" in sign language. If the two fingers are moved side to side, that's a "U" in sign language. If the little finger is straightened out, that's the letter "I" in sign language. If the pointer finger is straightened out instead of the little one, it's the letter "D."

Deaf people don't always spell out words letter by letter when they use sign language. One special sign can stand for a whole message. In sign language, pretending to throw a kiss means "thank you."

People everywhere use sign language even if they're not deaf. A person who uses their hands or body to get a message across, without talking, is using sign language. Shaking the head up and down means "yes." Shaking the head from side to side means "no." Sticking a tongue out is not a very nice message. Waving the hand instead of speaking is another way to say "goodbye" or "go away." These are ways sign language is used everyday.

Hearing-ear dogs can be taught sign language.

In this same way, dogs can also be taught sign language commands. Instead of speaking the command out loud, the deaf person uses a hand movement to get the message to the dog.

If the deaf person wants them to, many programs will teach hearing-ear dogs sign language. Signal Dogs at CCI are taught twelve different commands in sign language. It's part of their regular training.

Learning sounds

Sound awareness training comes next. Hearing-ear dogs perform most of their duties inside the home. So, many programs train the dogs in a real home setting. Some have record players or televisions turned on loudly. This gets the dog used to home noises. At the San Francisco program, there's even a house cat!

Training may start with the sound of an alarm clock. Many deaf people want their dog to wake them each morning. When the alarm goes off, the trainer runs with the dog on a leash to the clock. Then they run to another trainer who pretends to sleep on a bed. The dog is made to jump up and nuzzle the "sleeping" trainer.

The first trainer then runs with the dog back to the clock and then back to the sleeping trainer. This is done again and again. Finally, the sleeping trainer gets up and shuts off the alarm. The dog is rewarded with praise or given a food treat.

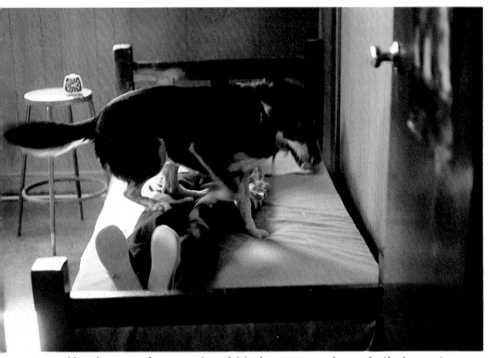

Hearing-ear dogs are taught to jump up and nuzzle their masters when an alarm clock goes off.

The dog is always trained to make contact with the sleeping trainer. It can be a touch of the paw or a nuzzle with the nose. Some smaller dogs are taught to jump on the bed and lick the trainer's face. The dog must not be too rough, but body contact is important. The dog is taught to keep alerting (running back and forth from the sound to the trainer) until the trainer gets out of bed and shuts off the alarm.

Once the dog learns to wake up the person while on the leash, the dog does it without the leash. The trainer always runs with the dog. Again and again they practice, until the dog gets it right. Most dogs enjoy this training. It's a fun-filled game for them.

Dogs are never punished for mistakes. But they're praised immediately when they do the right thing. The dogs are not taught to bark when alerting. The deaf person couldn't hear it.

Doorbells and other sounds

The doorbell is another everyday sound dogs can respond to. At the West Boylston, Massachusetts, Hearing-Ear Dog Program, the dogs are trained to alert their masters to doorbells of all kinds. They're also trained to respond to a knock at the door.

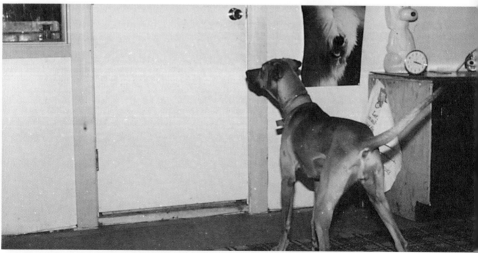

This hearing-ear dog is alerting to a knock on the door.

The training process for doorbells and knocks is the same as alerting to alarm clocks. With the dog on a leash, the trainer runs to the door when someone rings or knocks. Then they run to another trainer, who acts as the master. Back and forth they go, from the sound at the door to the master.

The dog is taught to nuzzle or jump up on the master. Once the dog catches on, they practice without the leash. The dog is trained to keep alerting until the master walks to the door. Then the dog is praised.

This same training method is used for oven timers, teakettles, smoke alarms, and teletypewriters. Teletypewriters are machines that can be attached to a deaf person's phone. The machine allows a deaf person to ''talk'' to other people who also have these machines. The machine prints out what the person on the other end is typing. These machines can also quickly get in touch with the police or fire department in an emergency.

Special sounds

Real objects are used in training whenever possible. However, one sound that is tape recorded is a baby crying. The tape recorder is then put next to a doll in a crib. The dog is trained to run back and forth between the doll and the master when it hears a crying sound.

The deaf person tells the trainers which special sounds

they want the dogs to alert them to. For example, a mother may ask that her dog be trained to respond to a baby crying or a child calling.

A deaf person who drives a car, or spends a lot of time outdoors, may request that the dog alert them to car horns and sirens. At West Boylston, Massachusetts, this training begins with the dog in the back seat of a car. When a siren or horn is heard, the dog is trained to put its paw on its master's shoulder. This doesn't interfere with driving, and the master is alerted to the sound. When walking outside together, a large dog is trained to step in front of its master when a horn or siren is heard. A smaller dog will jump up to get the master's attention.

Deaf people are taught to watch their dogs carefully when they go outside. Even if the dog is not trained to alert to horns or sirens, its ears will usually stand up if a sound has been heard. The deaf person is taught to look around to see where the noise is coming from, just to be safe.

Some programs train hearing-ear dogs to alert to prowlers. Whether they've been trained or not, the dogs may sense something is wrong and alert to strangers anyway. Others may begin barking to scare the prowler away. Some hearing-ear dogs alert to other dangers by instinct. Several have awakened their masters when they smelled leaking gas. This probably saved their master's life.

Hearing-ear dogs can be taught to be alert to the sound of a crying baby.

Meeting their masters

The last step in training is placing the animal with its new deaf master. Several programs have the deaf

Laurenda Owens and her new hearing-ear dog, Lulu.

person live at the training center for one to two weeks. They learn how to work with the dog as a team. Others will have a trainer deliver the dog to the deaf person's home. The trainer then works with them in the house for up to a week. A few programs do both of these things. Some also teach obedience and sound-response classes. The deaf person and the dog attend these classes together.

Deaf people who meet their dogs at the training center spend twenty-four hours a day with their dogs. The dogs sleep beside their beds at night. The new masters feed, bathe, brush, and play with the dogs everyday. The dog quickly learns to accept the deaf person as its new master.

When a dog is delivered to a deaf person's home, it takes several days for them to get close to each other. The dog will usually alert to the trainer the first few days. The trainer switches the dog's loyalty to the deaf person by doing less and less each day with the dog. The new master does more and more. He or she plays with, feeds, and takes care of the dog. Before long, the dog will run to its new master when it hears a sound.

Many hearing-ear dogs don't alert to sounds when there are hearing people at home. Somehow, they seem to know that they're only needed when the deaf person is alone. When the doorbell rings, some dogs ignore the sound and let a hearing person answer it. They take over again when the hearing people leave.

5.

Trainers

Each hearing-ear dog program has its own special requirements for choosing trainers. But all trainers are similar to each other in at least two ways. They love dogs, and they've had a lot of experience in training them.

Good trainers love working with dogs.

Ralph Dennard, Director of the San Francisco SPCA Program, trained dogs in his spare time. It was a hobby for twelve years before he made it his career. Most trainers get added happiness in saving homeless strays from the animal shelters. They also enjoy helping deaf people lead a normal life.

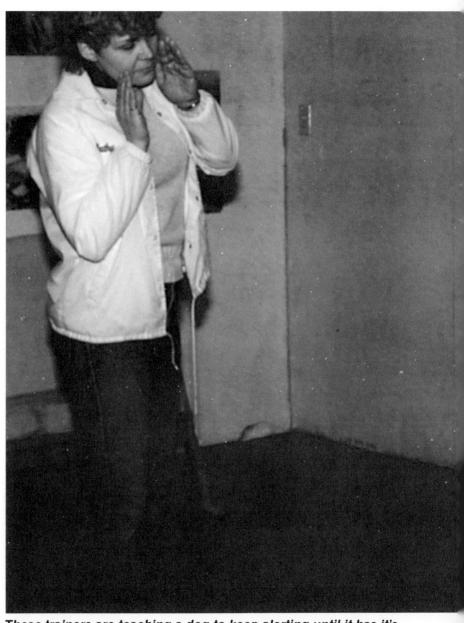

These trainers are teaching a dog to keep alerting until it has it's "master's" attention.

Who is eligible?

Not every deaf person can have a hearing-ear dog. Most programs require that the person be sixteen to eighteen years of age. Others will place dogs with younger people, depending on the case. In 1982, eight-year-old Jason Lufkin became the youngest person in the country to own a hearing-ear dog.

Only those with a very bad, or total, hearing loss can apply for a dog. Some programs will only accept those living alone or with other deaf people. Many require a fenced-in yard or a dog run. Some insist that there should be no other dogs in the home.

The deaf person must love and understand dogs. He or she must realize that the dog has to be exercised each day and given medical care. They must agree to continue to practice obedience and sound-response training at home.

Before a deaf person is given a dog, he or she is interviewed. Their home is then visited by a worker from the program. If the deaf person meets all requirements, they are placed on a waiting list. The dogs are then trained according to each person's special needs. Most hearing programs take three to six months before placing a dog with a deaf person. Others take as long as a year.

A graduate of a hearing-dog program receives his dog.

Michael and Jessica Petters and their hearing-ear dog, Deke.

Replacements and identification

If a dog dies, gets too old, or has a health problem, the deaf person can ask for a hearing-ear dog replacement. The program will then try to train and place another dog as soon as possible. If the program allows it, the older dog is often kept as a pet by the deaf owner.

All hearing-ear dogs wear bright orange collars and leashes. A special card is carried by deaf owners. The card states that the dog is a hearing-ear or signal dog. Nearly all states grant such dogs the right to go into hotels, restaurants, buses, trains, airplanes, and other public places.

The costs and benefits

It costs $3,000 to $5,000 (U.S.) to care for, train, and place a hearing-ear dog with a deaf person. Most programs are supported by private donations. People, service clubs, and businesses give money to help pay for expenses.

Many hearing-ear dog programs do not charge for the dogs. However, the deaf person is asked to give as much as they can to help pay the costs. A few programs charge small fees of $25 to $150 (U.S.). Private hearing-ear dog programs are like regular businesses. They require full payment for their services.

Aside from alerting deaf people to certain sounds, hearing-ear dogs help their owners in many other ways. For lonely people who live by themselves, a dog gives them something to care for. It keeps them busy. A strong bond of affection builds up between the dog and deaf person. By loving the dog, the person feels better about themself. Deaf people must take their dogs for walks. They get exercise and meet other people. They think less about their own deafness. Instead, they think more about having an active, happy life.

Since 1976, over two thousand dogs have been trained for hearing-ear work in the United States. At present, five hundred new dogs are added each year in programs all across the country. These dogs bring security and freedom to many lonely and anxious people. They bring love, help, and friendship to those living in silence.

Hearing-ear dogs have given love, help, and friendship to thou-sands of deaf people.

Glossary

ALERTING — *The way in which the dog gets the attention of its master; hearing-ear dogs jump up, nuzzle with their noses, or lick their masters, and then run back to the sound they're alerting to.*

BRINDLE — *A mixture of dark and light hairs; spotted or streaked with a dark color.*

CURIOSITY — *To want to learn about things, or know something.*

FAWN — *A yellowish-brown color.*

HEEL — *A term used in dog obedience training; when a dog walks closely along with the handler on the left side.*

INSTINCT — *Behavior that is automatic in animals; an inborn response or reaction.*

PUPPY SOCIALIZERS — *The people who play with, brush, and walk the dogs waiting to go to foster homes at Canine Companions for Independence in Santa Rosa, California.*

RUFF — *Long, thick hair around the neck.*

SABLE — *The color black or a very dark color.*

SIGN LANGUAGE — *The use of hand movements to communicate thoughts and ideas.*

SIGNAL DOGS — *The name used for hearing-ear dogs at Canine Companions for Independence in Santa Rosa, California.*

TELETYPEWRITERS — *Machines attached to telephones that print out what the person on the other end is typing; lets deaf people "talk" to others who have these machines.*

TEMPERAMENT — *The emotional characteristics that are special to each dog; its personality or frame of mind.*

VETERINARIAN — *A doctor who treats animals.*

READ ABOUT THE MANY KINDS
OF DOGS THAT WORK FOR A LIVING:

**HEARING-EAR
DOGS**

**GUIDE
DOGS**

**WATCH/GUARD
DOGS**

**LAW
ENFORCEMENT
DOGS**

**SEARCH
& RESCUE
DOGS**

**STUNT
DOGS**

**SLED
DOGS**

**MILITARY
DOGS**

CRESTWOOD HOUSE